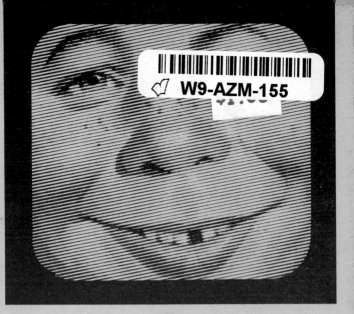

A MAD
LOOK AT TV

WRITTEN BY DICK DE BARTOLO
ILLUSTRATED BY ANGELO TORRES
EDITED BY NICK MEGLIN

WARNER BOOKS

A Warner Communications Company

Dedicated to Angelo Torres, without whose brilliant artwork this book would be awful.

Dick De Bartolo

Dedicated to Nick Meglin, without whose brilliant editing this book would be nothing.

Angelo Torres

Dedicated to Dick De Bartolo, without whose brilliant writing this book would be an awful nothing.

Nick Meglin

WARNER BOOKS EDITION

Copyright © 1974 by Dick De Bartolo,
Angelo Torres, and E.C. Publications, Inc.

ISBN: 0-446-94436-X

**Title "MAD" used with permission of
its owner, E.C. Publications, Inc.**

This Warner Books Edition is published by arrangement
with E.C. Publications, Inc.

Warner Books, Inc., 75 Rockefeller Plaza, New York, N.Y. 10019

Ⓦ A Warner Communications Company

Printed in the United States of America

First Printing: July, 1974

Reissued: July, 1980

10   9   8

CONTENTS

A moving chronicle of Doctors, Nurses,
Doctor's Aides, Nurse's Aides, Staff Members
—their lives, their hopes, their dreams,
their conflicts, their turmoil and their
inability to find parking space . . . oh, yeah,
and their patients—if there's time!

HOSPITAL STORY

6

7

8

9

11

13

14

15

17

21

23

28

29

31

33

35

Who is the most light-hearted (no matter how serious the subject may be) personality on TV? Why, the MC of any show like . . .

THE
JOHNNY TALK
SHOW

. . . and here's **Johnny!!**

41

43

46

47

THIS IS HOW YOU LIVED YOUR LIFE

52

53

55

59

Yes, Daisy, Dan was your childhood sweetheart, and the **first man** to ever propose to you! And you said **'no'**! Today Dan is worth over **half a million dollars!** His weekly income is over **$5,000!** He has a **Rolls Royce,** a **Cadillac,** and a **villa in Italy!** Yes, that's what you **threw away** 27 years ago, Daisy Starr when you made the **first fatal mistake** of your career and said 'no' to marrying Dr. Dan Finley! Doctor, I know you have to get back to your brain operation at the St. Help Us Hospital, in Syracuse, N.Y., 3,134 miles from here, so we'll let you go!

Bye, loser!

Yes, at 17 years of age, your life is already **running downhill!**
After high school, Daisy came to me and said she wanted to be a star! I taught her acting, singing, dancing and paid her way out to Hollywood!

In 1963 and 1964 you establish a new movie making record in Hollywood. In those two years you starred in **SMILE ON MY FACE; SONG IN MY HEART; PUCKER ON MY LIPS; KISS ON MY CHEEK;** and **TAP ON MY SHOES . . .**

Yes, it was a new movie making **record** alright! At the end of 1964, everyone who had the vaguest connection with any of those five films was **out of work!**

That's Gene Bianco, your **Internal Revenue Agent!** The I.R.S. has already **confiscated** the gold bracelet we give you as a memento of being on **THIS IS HOW YOU LIVE YOUR LIFE!** Yes, Daisy, you're in **debt** up to your **eye-balls,** living **beyond** your means, your home is a **shambles,** your personal life is a **shambles,** and your two illigitimate children **loathe you!** In short, you find that life is **not a bowl of cherries . . .**

But then we decided to see if Daisy Starr could handle the lead in a new major motion picture! She co-starred with **Sir Lawrence Olivia, Sir John Guilgood, Helen Hayze,** and **Lynn Fontaine** . . . and Daisy turned in the **best performance** of her **entire life!!**

Why that's producer **John Chevy!**

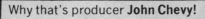

John we're all looking forward to seeing Daisy's **comeback** on the silver screen!!
Well, you're going to have to **wait a long time,** because after appearing on this **cheap, corny, pseudo-sentimental** T V show, we decided she doesn't **belong** with the likes of **Sir Lawrence Olivia, Sir John Guilgood, Helen Hayze,** and **Lynn Fontaine!** We're going to **edit** her **out** of the picture!

This book now pauses for a station break!
          THIS IS
     "A MAD LOOK AT T.V."
And no station break is complete without
at least ONE commercial . . .

79

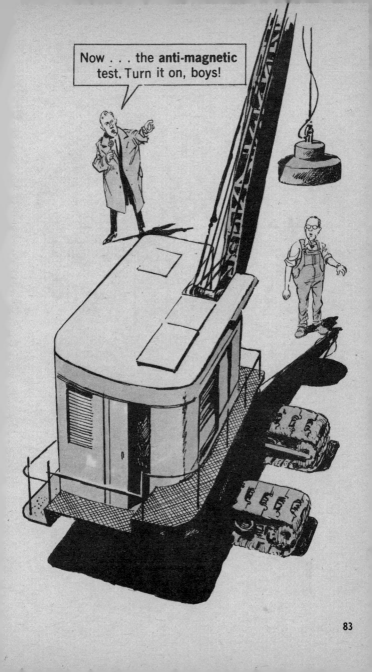

83

PLINK

CLINK

PING

85

What makes a situation comedy funny? The plot? No! The lines? *Never!*

It's THE LAUGH TRACK!

Dedicated to the proposition that all TV viewers are created equally stupid, and that we don't know what's funny and have to be shown where we should laugh, network producers and directors came up with the laugh track. As always, use quickly became over-use, and abuse was the logical end product. Lines that weren't even designed for a laugh soon brought down the house by the simple turning of a knob.

Let's take a look at a typical situation comedy *without* the laugh track . . .

SHE'S A DILLY

STARRING
SANDRA SHLOCK
AS DILLY

WITH
DAME JOY WESSEL
AS MISS PRINKLE
AND
"SKIP" CLASSES
AS FREDDIE

TONIGHT'S SHOW:
"The Postman Always
Scrounges Twice"

91

. . . and, like that! Ah, but with the *laugh track*, what is merely stupid and banal becomes hilarious and side-splitting! Let's turn up the knob to full amplification and start the reel over . . .

HAHAHAHAHA

94

TITTER TITTER

CHUCKLE GUFFAW

HO HO HEE HEE

TITTER TITTER

103

TITTER TITTER

CHUCKLE GUFFAW

GUFFAW GUFFAW

114

YOUR BUDDIES
AND THE NEWS

122

123

125

127

128

130

132

133

135

136

137

EAT YOUR HEART OUT

Good evening, ladies and gentlemen! I'm Jimmy Wholesome welcoming you to America's favorite give-away show——**Eat Your Heart Out!** Tonight, some members of our studio audience will **win prizes** that will make this the **happiest moment** of his or her life! Some others will also win prizes, but in a **fit of greed** to get **more,** will **lose everything,** making it the **worst night** of his or her life! But that's show biz! Now let's meet our fun-loving M.C. FRED FLAKEY . . .

141

Well, **how do you like that!** That lady **wasn't** kidding! She wasn't one of your typical, **idle boasters!** I've got **great respect** for that type of person! Announcer Jimmy Wholesome, how about a prize for this nice, **dead lady?**

Sure, Fred! A Hawaian vacation for **two!** Yes, the dead lady's husband will travel first class on a 747 and stay at the lush Blue Paradise Hotel! The dead lady will fly in the same 747, in the cargo area, laid out in this elegant, hand-carved mahogany-effect fiberglass coffin by Bye-Bye Baby Slumber Box—a prize worth approximately $3,476.89 from **Eat Your Heart Out!**

BANG

143

144

145

146

147

148

149

151

But **you,** young lady, just because you're **empty-headed,** don't go home **empty-handed!** We know you're a little depressed because you thought for a minute there that you had won $24,756.90 in prizes, plus the chance to go for our **SUPER BONUS CHEST** which is worth tonight over 139 million dollars!! But we want you to **have something**—so here's a brand new movie projector, plus a film showing you **losing** your **chance** at the prizes and the **SUPER BONUS CHEST!!** Now anytime you feel like it you can show this wonderful film and **EAT YOUR HEART OUT!!**

153

156

157

159

Yes, but your "companion" decided to make that **her** choice, and Mary Ames, there can only be **one** big winner, but we don't want you to go home empty handed, so you can have the picture on the right worth 1.98, plus the satisfaction of knowing you have a "best friend" who owns an original painting worth $2 million.

If she shows me that painting I'll **break it over her head!**

160

EAT YOUR HEART OUT Mary Ames! And now it's the moment everyone's been waiting for . . . **THE SUPER BONUS CHESTS** worth tonight over 139 million dollars! Now let's meet our two **big winners** of the evening, Chrissy Curtis and Frank Adduci . . .

164

165

166

168

FRONTIER
FRAMUS

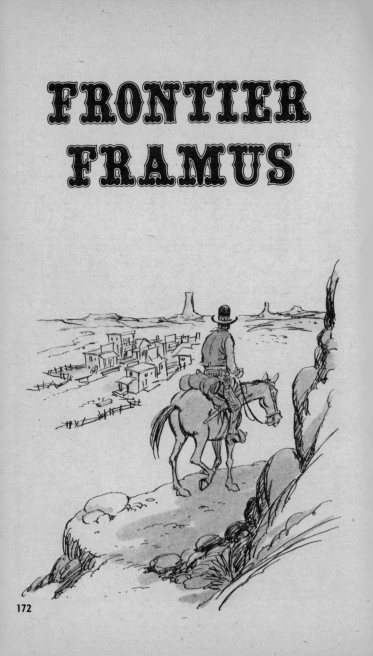

173

174

175

182

187

189

190

THE END